Birthing the Integrity Within You
Corporate America Edition

By: Shanesha Scott

All rights reserved

No part of this book may be reproduced, stored in a retrieval system, or transmitted in any form or by any means, electronic, mechanical, photocopying, recording, or otherwise, without express written permission of the publisher.

Cover design by: Giovanni Misanrande
Photo Cover: Deon Casey Photography

Table of Contents

Dedication 5

Preface 7

Chapter 1: What is Integrity? 11

Chapter 2: The Landscape of Corporate America 14

Chapter 3: Developing Integrity Across All Levels 16

Chapter 4: The Role of Leadership in Upholding Integrity 19

Chapter 5: Navigating Ethical Dilemmas 21

Chapter 6: The Cost of Compromise 25

Chapter 7: Understanding Workplace Bullying and Discrimination ... 28

Chapter 8: Diversity, Equity, & Inclusion: A Matter of Integrity 31

Chapter 9: Institutionalized Racism in Corporate America 35

Chapter 10: The Role of Whistleblowers 39

Chapter 11: Human Resources Ethical Compass 41

Chapter 12: Building a Culture of Integrity 46

Chapter 13: The Future of Integrity in Corporate America 49

Chapter 14: Taking Action 53

Chapter 15: My Final Thoughts As An I/O Psychologist 56

References 59

About the Author 64

Dedication

This book is dedicated to all those who have endured the silent struggles of workplace bullying, discrimination, and harassment. Your stories of resilience and courage have profoundly impacted me. I am deeply grateful for the trust you have placed in me by sharing your journeys. May this work serve as a testament to your strength and be an inspiration for change, equality, understanding, and compassion in every workplace.

Preface

As an ethical leader in corporate America and an industrial and organizational psychologist, integrity is not just a principle I adhere to but my driving force. With employees facing hostile work environments, discrimination, and harassment, I have seen firsthand the profound impact of leaders who lack integrity. These issues are not just abstract ideas; they manifest in employees' everyday lives and significantly influence their work experiences. Regrettably, these experiences can take a toll on their mental health and hinder their career growth. As I pen this preface, I feel a overwhelming personal responsibility to highlight the urgency of addressing these challenges for the well-being of employees and the health of these organizations.

Throughout my career, particularly these last five years, I have encountered situations where leadership and human resources, the entities designed to advocate for employees, have been complicit in perpetuating toxic and hostile work environments. I have seen leaders prioritize personal relationships over the collective well-being of employees, allowing toxic and discriminatory behaviors to thrive unchecked. The victims are often made to look like the problem, and the silence surrounding bullying and discrimination is indisputable. This has left me feeling that the people in power all share the same sentiments—championing an environment where fear and biases are the rules that are encouraged and not the exception that is frowned upon.

It is disheartening to realize how often those in positions of authority abuse their power and overlook and minimize the experiences of marginalized and targeted employees. Often, leadership and human resources are in alliance to protect the toxic leader and advocate for an unhealthy work environment. This failure not only undermines employee trust but also erodes the very foundations of a productive workplace. I have watched talented individuals (myself included) leave organizations by getting "pushed out" (made to go unwillingly) or wrongfully terminated. This is not because of their capabilities or talent as an employee but because they were the next victim of the toxic leader or they could no longer endure the system that failed to uphold the values of respect and integrity.

This book is a call to action. I intend to raise awareness of these issues by sharing my honest experiences. I also provide best practices to keep your integrity intact, even when it involves a friend or when it seems like the corporate machine is against you. I urge leaders, human resources professionals, employee relations, and legal departments within organizations to recognize the importance of upholding integrity and encouraging an inclusive and respectful workplace free from toxicity, biases, and discrimination.

I am confronting the uncomfortable truth of how the lack of integrity often leads to workplace bullying, favoritism, and discrimination, all compromising organizations at the highest levels. Organizations can begin to dismantle these toxic practices and push for ethical leadership who encourages integrity. Every individual deserves a psychologically safe workplace. All I ask of you is to keep an open mind. Do not discount people's experiences. Often, toxic leaders who lack integrity subtly victimize their employees. They may be well respected, but behind closed doors, the victims are going through a silent hell. I also ask you to participate in the movement toward change. Together, we can redefine the standards of integrity, ethics, and morality in our workplaces, ensuring that everyone is valued and respected. Take this journey toward a more equitable and compassionate corporate culture where integrity is not just a principle but a lived reality.

Chapter 1: What is Integrity?

Integrity in and outside corporate America is a commitment to doing what is right, even when no one is watching. It demonstrates honesty, transparency, and accountability in all business transactions. This commitment starkly contrasts the facade some people put on, where their true, awful character is revealed when unobserved. In the workplace, this can show up as a leader who lacks transparency in their decision-making, mistreats employees based on who they are, and lets personal biases influence their actions.

Integrity has different dimensions, including honesty, ethical behavior, and accountability. Integrity is an important characteristic of ethics and virtue in organizations, which is also measured as an adage in leadership effectiveness (Ete et al., 2022). Having honesty signifies being truthful in your words and actions. In leadership, people often throw honesty out the door once they have this title and a position of authority. Leaders need to realize that honesty builds trust. Trust is a key element in building relationships with employees and clients alike. Trustworthiness is also a key component and encompasses benevolence. Benevolence entails the sense of helpfulness a leader has towards their followers regarding loyalty and concern (Colquitt & Baer, 2023). People are more likely to respect an honest person. This also showcases reliability, all of which assist in open communication and a work environment that will thrive.

Ethical behavior goes hand in hand with integrity. Ethics is a theoretical word derived from the Greek word *ethos*, which means character or custom (Sims, 1992). Ethical behavior involves adhering to moral principles and standards that govern our actions. This means avoiding wrongdoings and actively making decisions that reflect fairness and respect for others. There have been times that I have observed leaders acting unethically and moving the goalpost based on who their friends were or, unfortunately, having biases based on race, which impacted all elements of the job. Although I spoke up when I saw these unethical practices, they often fell upon deaf ears. Eventually, I was pushed out of an organization I started and retaliated against. My experiences have only strengthened the urgency to raise awareness in driving change. It is not enough to know what is right; we must actively work to make it a reality in the workplace.

Accountability ties everything together. Where there is integrity, there is responsibility for one's decisions and potential consequences for unethical actions. Accountability is about taking responsibility for your actions and decisions. It is a key aspect of integrity in leadership, as it shows that a leader is willing to stand by their choices and their team. I have seen no accountability for some leaders wreaking havoc behind the scenes. Even when an employee goes up the proper chain of command, it falls upon deaf ears, and the leader is not held accountable. This means owning up to and learning from your mistakes instead of deflecting, lying, blaming others, or making excuses. We are all human and make mistakes, but it is important to remember that these mistakes can be valuable learning opportunities. It is problematic when a mistake turns into a pattern and a leader starts abusing their position of authority. When integrity is upheld, it ultimately reinforces trust. When people see that you stand by your commitments and acknowledge when things go awry, they are more likely to feel secure in your character.

Integrity is not just a single trait but an active interchange between honesty, ethical behavior, and accountability. Living with integrity means consistently aligning your actions with your values, being truthful, and taking responsibility—forming a solid foundation for respectful and meaningful relationships within your team, organization, and clients. Ethical behavior is not just a choice but necessary for building strong and connected relationships.

Chapter 2:
The Landscape of Corporate America

In this new era of corporate America, the rules are evolving faster than ever. The landscape is no longer solely defined by profits but by a new currency that is more valuable than gold: integrity. This major shift is driven by digital transformation, the need for social responsibility, and a demand for authenticity. It is steering stakeholders away from the traditional 'boys' club culture' and 'brogrammer culture,' a term used to describe a work environment that is male-dominated and often hostile to women, as they pose a financial risk (Miazad, 2020). As companies navigate the complexities of remote work, shifting consumer expectations, and heightened scrutiny, the emphasis on ethical practices has never been more significant. This includes the inner workings of corporations.

The current corporate America landscape is characterized by a complex exchange of rapid transformation and rising expectations, particularly regarding integrity. When companies rise to meet these demands, stakeholders and employees are not just respected but empowered, influencing and shaping the corporate landscape. Conversely, a leader may display Machiavellianism and narcissism and use people for their gain. The latter is a common theme often seen among leaders. How are employees being treated? How is leadership conducting themselves? These are questions organizations need to ask themselves. This is a moment when transparency and accountability go hand in hand for survival and progress within an organization. Companies are increasingly held accountable for their actions, making integrity a value necessary for survival. There is a strong push for corporate social responsibility, which goes beyond mere compliance with laws and regulations. It requires organizations to consider their impact on society and the environment in all aspects of their operations, from supply chain management to product development, moving beyond mere compliance to genuine accountability.

Transparency has become paramount in building trust. Organizations that communicate openly about their practices and decisions are more likely to earn stakeholder confidence. Companies are expected to uphold ethical standards and comply with evolving laws as regulatory scrutiny increases- especially around environmental and social governance. In this environment, employees play an integral role in maintaining integrity as part of the corporate structure. Their engagement and well-being are emphasized, highlighting their value in the corporate landscape. Finally, businesses that respond with honesty and empathy can reinforce their reputation in times of crisis, reassure stakeholders, and instill confidence. At the same time, those who fail to act ethically may face serious repercussions. Overall, integrity has emerged as a foundational element in navigating the challenges and opportunities of today's corporate landscape. At the same time, toxic leadership and HR practices are being talked about at a rapid pace due to the power of social media. Organizations can no longer sweep toxicity and discriminatory practices under the rug without them eventually getting exposed. This is a win for employees of these organizations.

Chapter 3:
Developing Integrity Across All Levels

Integrity is not merely a characteristic of a few individuals within an organization; but a collective responsibility that unites us at every level. People inspired by values are more likely to act with integrity than those governed by rules (Mariscotti, 2020). When we think about integrity, it is easy to associate it with leadership or those in authoritative positions. However, the truth is that every employee plays a crucial role in promoting a culture of integrity. From the newest intern to an experienced executive, each person is part of a shared mission to influence the ethical landscape of their workplace. Motivated employees also work better and treat clients well (Mariscotti, 2020). I have witnessed the team morale tank when the culture is toxic and lacks integrity. Creating an environment where everyone feels that their voice matters and their actions contribute to a larger purpose is integral to a healthy work environment.

To cultivate this culture, organizations must actively encourage open communication and create safe channels for employees to express their concerns. A solid ethical culture influences employees' behavior (Mariscotti, 2020). These channels should be secure and confidential, making employees feel safe and confident in raising their concerns. Empowering individuals to speak up against unethical practices is not just a policy on paper; it is a fundamental shift in workplace dynamics. Employees need to know that their input is valued and that they will not face repercussions for raising concerns.

This can be achieved through regular training sessions emphasizing the importance of integrity and recognizing and rewarding those who demonstrate ethical behavior. When employees understand that they can contribute to a culture of integrity, they are more likely to act in ways that align with the organization's values, ultimately championing a more substantial, more ethical workplace for everyone.

Leadership sets the tone for the entire organization. Leaders should model integrity in their actions, decisions, and communications. Employees are encouraged to follow suit when executives demonstrate ethical behavior and uphold company values. The key to this is transparency in decision-making processes, which not only reassures but also instills confidence in the team. Organizations should have clear core values and ethical standards clearly defined and readily available to all employees. Ethics assists in reflecting on the individual's behavior and whether the behavior was good or bad (Mariscotti, 2020). This includes developing comprehensive policies outlining behavior, decision-making, and accountability expectations. By communicating these values consistently, employees at all levels understand what integrity looks like within the organization.

Integrity must be a shared responsibility across all levels of the organization. John Zenger and Joseph Folkman, who are renowned professionals in performance and leadership, have said, "In organizations with integrity, great emphasis is placed on honesty and ethical behavior. Success is not only in terms of achieving results but also considering how to get them (Mariscotti, 2020)." Clear accountability must ensure that all employees, including leadership, are held to the same standards. When ethical breaches occur, addressing them swiftly and fairly demonstrates a commitment to integrity. However, this does not happen in some cases. When leaders have inside connections or are friends with people in HR, everyone "turns a blind eye." This is a vicious cycle that will, unfortunately, continue for years with no end in sight.

Organizations should proactively and regularly assess their integrity practices and policies to ensure they remain effective and relevant. By gathering employee feedback and conducting integrity audits, you can identify areas for improvement and reinforce a commitment to ethical behavior. Having a proactive approach instead of a reactive approach helps to cultivate a culture of integrity that permeates every level—from leadership to HR to employees. When integrity is prioritized, it not only enhances the workplace environment but also builds a strong foundation for long-term success and sustainability.

Chapter 4: The Role of Leadership in Upholding Integrity

Leaders have a fundamental responsibility to model integrity within their organizations. Leaders who demonstrate ethical behavior set the tone for the entire team. This means being honest, transparent, and accountable in their actions. Social scientists outline position power as the likely influence derived from the employees' role in the organization, while personal power is the possible influence derived from the employees' characteristics and some parts of the relationship (Colquitt & Baer, 2023). Behavioral integrity is vital in the leader-follower and organizational-follower relationships (Ete, 2020). In an environment of toxicity or discrimination, trust is lost. Employees often look to their leaders for guidance, and when they see integrity in action, it encourages them to adopt similar values. Leaders should prioritize integrity since their actions significantly impact the team's trust and create an environment where ethical practices can thrive. This responsibility goes beyond mere compliance with rules; it promotes a culture where everyone feels responsible and accountable to act with integrity.

An organization's leadership style plays a key role in shaping its culture of integrity. Research shows that effective leadership is significant in creating a safe and supportive environment within a company (Nasim, 2023). For example, democratic or transformational leadership styles facilitate open communication and teamwork, nurturing a strong ethical culture. When leaders actively seek out their team's input and genuinely value their perspectives, it fosters a sense of ownership and accountability among employees. On the flip side, authoritarian or transactional leadership can stifle communication and discourage ethical conduct. In these environments, employees might feel compelled to prioritize outcomes over integrity, which can allow unethical practices to take place. This highlights the need for promoting democratic leadership, as it encourages ethical behavior and cultivates a transparent and healthy workplace culture.

Thankfully, all hope is not lost. Some leaders have successfully prioritized ethical behavior and made integrity a cornerstone of their leadership. Case in point- Paul Polman, former CEO of Unilever, is known for his commitment to sustainability and ethical business practices. He emphasized long-term value over short-term profits and encouraged his team to consider the broader impact of their decisions on society and the environment. His leadership improved Unilever's reputation and inspired others to adopt similar ethical standards, contributing to a better society and a healthier environment. Leaders who demonstrate how prioritizing integrity improves their organizations' reputations and inspire others to adopt similar ethical standards.

Chapter 5:
Navigating Ethical Dilemmas

Dealing with ethical dilemmas is a personal challenge for employees in corporate settings. Lefkowitz defined ethical dilemmas as an evaluation of moral or ethical quality that is dependent on an individual's perception and assessed individual observations of why the situation was ethical; it must also be considered how status and victim characteristics would have influenced the reports provided in the central article (Thornton-Lugo & Cubrich, 2021). The pressure to meet targets or align with company goals can sometimes conflict with personal values, leading to common ethical dilemmas. These include handling conflicts of interest, dealing with dishonest practices, and facing pressure to compromise quality or safety standards. Employees may be torn between what is right and what is expected of them, creating significant stress and uncertainty. However, ethical capabilities, the most promising theory in ethical behavior, provides a reassuring framework. Research has shown that it acknowledges the relationship between leadership characteristics, behaviors, and organizational effectiveness (JRC et al., 2010), instilling employee confidence about the potential for ethical behavior to enhance organizational effectiveness.

A clear agenda is invaluable for guiding employees in making ethical decisions. As Peikoff suggests, principles serve a dual purpose in guiding decision-makers through complex choices toward long-term goals. They help project the future and aid in choosing alternatives (Woiceshyn, 2011). Organizations can utilize an ethical decision-making model, as seen below, which will guide the organization and its individuals.

Ethical Decision-Making Model

- *Integrity* is about being honest and consistent in your values and actions. It means doing the right thing, even when no one is watching.
- *Accountability*: Taking responsibility for your decisions is crucial. This trait emphasizes owning up to the outcomes of your choices and being willing to stand by them.
- *Fairness*: Consider all sides of any issue and ensure everyone is treated fairly. Avoid biases at all costs.
- *Transparency*: Being open about your decision-making process strenghtens trust. Transparency involves sharing information and being clear about how decisions are made.
- *Respect:* Valuing the opinions and rights of others is vital. This trait encourages listening to different perspectives and treating everyone with dignity.
- *Courage*: Making ethical decisions often requires courage, especially when facing pressure to act otherwise. It is about standing firm in your beliefs, even when difficult.
- *Empathy*: Understanding how your decisions affect others helps create a more compassionate approach. Empathy allows you to see things from other people's viewpoints.

- *Ethical Communication*: Leaders that foster open and transparent communication. It is encouraged to provide honest and ethical communication within the organization where relevant information is shared (Bizadmin, 2023).

These traits collectively contribute to a strong ethical decision-making process, helping individuals and organizations navigate multifaceted dilemmas with confidence and integrity.

Organizations should appoint a risk manager, which is a critical component in developing an ethical decision-making model. This model provides employees with the necessary guidance to identify the correct course of action. The organizational framework involves assessing the facts of a situation, identifying alternatives and potential consequences of each option, selecting the best course of action, implementing the decision, and evaluating the results (Zablow, 2006). Many organizations also establish confidential hotlines and websites. These ethics helplines are designed to assist employees in navigating ethical dilemmas. To ensure employees feel comfortable in reporting potential ethical violations, the confidentiality and integrity of these hotlines and sites should always be upheld (Zablow, 2006). Decisions made through these methods will provide employees with the necessary guidance and allow employees to ensure that their choices align with their values and the organization's ethical standards.

Facing an ethical dilemma at work can be particularly challenging when a leader demonstrates biases and discrimination. Imagine an employee constantly witnessing their leader favoring certain team members based on personal connections rather than merit. This happens often, and I have seen it firsthand. This also can manifest in promotions, project assignments, and everyday interactions, leaving others feeling undervalued and marginalized. This personally happened to me. A toxic leader wanted their friend in my position and often left me off of important projects, so in essence, sabotaging my career growth and also creating a narrative that I was not competent enough to be on these decision-making projects. Imagine being in a situation where you notice your manager consistently showing favoritism towards certain team members and makes decisions that are heavily biased. You are faced with a tough choice: do you speak up and confront your leader about this unfair treatment, possibly putting your position at risk? Or do you stay silent, allowing this discriminatory and unethical behavior to persist? This predicament challenges your values and courage and sheds light on how such leadership behavior can affect the entire workplace environment and team morale. Navigating this ethical dilemma will allow you to weigh the potential consequences for your colleagues, the organization, and your sense of integrity. Victims of bullying and discrimination often remain silent due to fear of retaliation. I remained silent for years and my mental health suffered. Ultimately, leaders should act with integrity, upholding the organization's values, which inspires employees to do the same, creating an inclusive environment for everyone.

Chapter 6:
The Cost of Compromise

Lacking integrity in the workplace can lead to many risks and consequences that affect the organization and its employees and stakeholders. When ethical standards are compromised, the fallout will be noteworthy and long-lasting. Behavioral integrity (BI) was first presented by Bauman Simons in 2002, which refers to BI as the supposed pattern of alignment with a person's words and deeds (Sims, 1992). Leadership within these organizations has become hypocrites in nature. Employee surveys and policies and procedures are in place; however, when an employee presents a potential ethical violation, human resources and other leaders fail to do anything about it. This often results in the victim feeling helpless, and frequently, the victims are retaliated against. Behavioral integrity is important within modern organizations that function in a self-motivated environment because leaders are challenged to act consistently in word and deed. At the same time, employees need certainty and predictability (Sims, 1992). When integrity falls by the wayside, companies are at a high risk of failing.

Enron is a notable company that eventually failed due to widespread accounting fraud. Enron underwent financialization, which changed its priorities in the practice of new capitalism. Enron eventually followed Wall Street's lead and put high value on shareholder value (Arcadi, 2020). When the truth came out, Enron filed for bankruptcy, and tens of thousands of jobs were lost. The immediate impact was catastrophic, and employee morale plummeted. Employees were betrayed, and many lost their entire life savings. This situation highlights the detrimental effects of unethical behavior on an organization's culture, ultimately eroding employees' trust in the organization and its leaders. When the people in charge lack integrity, entire organizations will eventually fail in some aspect.

The long-term impacts of lacking integrity are profound. The revelation of unethical practices can severely damper employee morale. The wrong leader can cause a substantial drop in self-confidence. Team meetings that were once animated and filled with camaraderie, ideas, and opinions turn into silent gatherings. Employee survey scores, once excelling, can plummet into failure. This would be a red flag for an industrial and organizational (I/O) psychologist like myself. It is of the utmost importance to recognize these signs and address them immediately. Ask questions like What are driving these results? Workers are less likely to feel proud to work for their organization which leads to disengagement and higher turnover rates. In an environment where integrity is not present, collaboration will suffer as employees may become cautious of one another, fearing that their colleagues also engage in dishonest behavior. It is important to recognize that integrity is needed for effective collaboration, as it builds trust and respect amongst team members.

As seen in Enron's case, the company's reputation is another casualty. Once trust is lost, it can take years, if not decades, to rebuild. Stakeholders, customers, and potential employees are likely to think twice before associating with a company with a tainted reputation.

This loss of trust can lead to decreased customer loyalty, impacting sales and profits. Financial performance is significantly affected by legal fees, fines, and settlements that can deplete resources. Additionally, negative publicity can hinder new business opportunities. It is important to understand that the long-term effects of reputation loss can be severe, making it even more important for companies to prioritize integrity and ethical practices to avoid such risks.

The risks of lacking integrity in the workplace are significant. Cases like Enron serve as stark reminders of the serious repercussions that unethical behavior can have on employee morale, company reputation, and financial health. On the other hand, organizations that emphasize integrity can create a more positive workplace culture and attain long-term success, highlighting the lasting advantages of maintaining ethical standards.

Chapter 7: Understanding Workplace Bullying and Discrimination

This chapter is near and dear to my heart as I experienced workplace bullying and discrimination for four years. The trauma I endured daily left me with anxiety, depression, and PTSD. It impacted me so much that I decided to get my master's degree in industrial and organizational psychology in efforts to positively change organizational culture and behaviors. I decided to include this chapter in this book in order to provide a lived experience of how this egregious behavior can manifest when leaders and organizations systematically lack integrity. Turning this tragedy into triumph, I found an amazing organization I now partner with called End Workplace Abuse (EWA). EWA champions psychologically safe workplaces and currently has legislation on the table to pass the Workplace Psychological Safety Act (WPSA) in all 50 states. This partnership has been transformative for me and many others who have experienced similar traumas. It has given us hope and optimism for a future with psychologically safe workplaces. If you have experienced workplace trauma and would like to know more about EWA, please visit www.endworkplaceabuse.com.

Workplace bullying refers to persistent, harmful behaviors directed at an individual or group, creating a hostile work environment. This can include verbal abuse, sabotaging work, spreading rumors, or isolating someone. Discrimination, on the other hand, involves unfair treatment of individuals based on characteristics such as race, gender, age, religion, or disability. Dealing with toxic leaders can lead to a range of physical health issues for employees. Employees might struggle with sleep disturbances, weight changes, digestive problems, headaches, and hair loss. On the emotional and psychological side, the impact can be just as severe, causing a drop in self-confidence, heightened anxiety, and even depression (Khan et al., 2022). Both issues undermine the principle of integrity, which emphasizes fairness, respect, and ethical behavior. When bullying or discrimination occurs, it diminishes trust and damages the moral fabric of an organization.

Workplace bullying and discrimination are unfortunately common in many corporate settings. Bullying is about domination, which includes dehumanization, degrading, and devaluing (Carle, 2023). Studies have shown that a significant percentage of employees have experienced or witnessed bullying, while discrimination based on identity factors remains a prevalent issue. I have seen situations where there were clear instances of biases and discrimination, but the toxic leader was heavily protected while the victims were made to look like problems. Honestly, going through this situation myself and also seeing this toxic leader bully and discriminate against others truly opened my eyes to the inner workings of corporate America. It has been a valuable lesson learned and turned me off in a huge way. The impact on my mental health has been alarming. I never thought that going to work to make a living to provide for my family would end up leaving me depressed and filled with anxiety—so many sleepless nights and PTSD. The impact of these problems is profound, and they can lead to decreased employee morale, increased turnover, and a decline in productivity. Furthermore, organizations may face reputational damage and potential legal consequences, which can hinder their ability to attract and retain top talent. We all must become more aware of these issues and take action to create a healthier, more inclusive workplace.

Leadership and human resources are key players in tackling workplace bullying and discrimination. Leaders set the tone for organizational culture and must demonstrate a commitment to integrity by promoting inclusivity and respect. Employers often only look at how bullying may impact them from a legal perspective or if it will cost the organization financially, which can lead to the failure of the employers' policies (Carbo, 2017). This includes implementing clear policies against bullying and discrimination, providing training, and encouraging open communication. Human resources need to keep a close eye on the workplace atmosphere and be ready to address any complaints with care. By fostering an environment where employees feel comfortable speaking up, organizations can begin to tackle these issues head-on and advocate for a healthier work environment. Human resources must actively follow their policies and procedures for this to work.

Chapter 8: Diversity, Equity, & Inclusion: A Matter of Integrity

When I reflect on the role of diversity, equity, and inclusion (DEI) in shaping the future of corporate America, I am reminded by how these concepts are deeply rooted with integrity. DEI has emerged as a key element in creating an inclusive culture in corporate America, not only shaping the workplace culture but also the integrity of organizations. The integration of DEI into this equation adds an important layer, transforming integrity from a static notion into a practice that is constantly evolving and adapting to our diverse world. So, what exactly is DEI? Here's DEI defined by DEI experts from ABC News:

- *Diversity* refers to the representation of individuals from an assortment of backgrounds, including people from different races, genders, sexual orientations, religions, and disabilities.
- *Equity* focuses on fairness and justice, particularly compensation and whether individuals are being paid and treated equally.
- *Inclusion* is about whether individuals feel like they belong and whether they feel heard and valued (Alfonseca, 2023).

Imagine walking into your corporate office where the walls are decorated with art from many cultures, the workforce reflects the community it serves, and every voice is not just heard but appreciated and valued. This is the heart of a diverse and inclusive work environment, where everyone feels a sense of belonging. When employees feel represented, they are more likely to engage authentically and contribute meaningfully to the company's mission. This reality nurtures a culture of honesty and trust, which are indispensable components of integrity. When individuals from various backgrounds collaborate, they bring unique perspectives that challenge the status quo and encourages ethical decision-making.

Diversity brings a wealth of perspectives and experiences to the table. I've seen firsthand how teams with diverse backgrounds spark innovative ideas and solutions. When I work alongside colleagues from different cultures, genders, and life experiences, I find that our discussions are more productive and insightful. This diversity enhances creativity and helps us better understand and serve our diverse customer base. I also recognize that DEI initiatives can significantly impact an organization's response to challenges. Without these initiatives, people of color and other protected classes may face discrimination or more subtle acts of hostility called microaggressions (Schreane, 2021).

In my experience, companies prioritizing diversity and inclusion tend to navigate crises more effectively. Even if an offense may be legal, ethical leaders still frown upon offensive behaviors (Schreane, 2021). These leaders are equipped to recognize these offensive behaviors and can rectify these situations immediately. Having diverse voices in decision-making contributes to a more balanced approach, allowing leaders to make decisions that reflect the values of integrity and accountability. It's clear that embracing diversity is not just a smart business plan but also an ethical choice that organizations should be committed to, leading to innovative ideas and a better understanding of their employees and customers.

The impact that DEI has on integrity extends beyond the internal dynamics of an organization. DEI also influences how companies interact with their communities. Organizations prioritizing a diverse workforce are more likely to understand and address the needs of their clientele, leading to better products and services. This understanding not only promotes corporate social responsibility, a key aspect of DEI but also significantly impacts community relations. When companies act with integrity, acknowledging and addressing social issues, they not only build stronger relationships with stakeholders but also contribute to the betterment of society as a whole. On a personal level, working in an organization that prioritizes DEI made me feel more fulfilled and motivated. Even though the organization may not uphold its policies and procedures, knowing that I am committed to fostering an equitable environment inspires me to uphold those values in my own work. Leaders and HR personnel may have biases and not uphold these standards. Erica Foldy, a professor at NYU's Wagner Graduate School of Public Service, and Tina Opie, a DEI consultant and professor at Babson College, believe critics of DEI often frame DEI initiatives as unfairly giving something to marginalized people who some say "have not earned" it and are taking things away from others (Alfonseca, 2023). "Dominance and privilege – understandably, those things are hard to give up," Foldy said. An example of these sentiments from Texas Governor Greg Abbott and Florida Governor Ron DeSantis has stirred up controversy, with Abbott saying to state representatives that

DEI initiatives are illegal. DeSantis said that DEI is an indoctrinating program and, in 2021, announced the "Stop WOKE" Act. This bill would have restricted race-related curricula in schools, workplaces, and higher education institutions. A federal judge has since blocked the bill from affecting higher education (Alfonseca, 2023).

The role of diversity, equity, and inclusion in corporate America is not just about maintaining the status quo. I believe these foundational elements have the power to transform, enhance integrity, promote a positive workplace culture, and push for ethical practices. As organizations continue to navigate the complexities of the modern business environment, prioritizing DEI will be essential in building a future where integrity is not just an ideal but a lived reality for every employee and stakeholder, ushering in a new era of corporate culture.

Chapter 9: Institutionalized Racism in Corporate America

As a child, I was always told that if I worked hard, I would reap the benefits of having the life I deserve. This advice, while true in some aspects, carries a different weight for a Black woman like myself and many others in marginalized communities. Stepping into the corporate world, I soon discovered that hard work alone is not always enough, especially for marginalized people. In these moments, I witnessed the incredible resilience of individuals who, despite the odds, continue to push forward.

Institutionalized racism was first coined by Stokely Carmichael (later known as Kwame Ture) and Charles Hamilton in their landmark publication Black Power: The Politics of Liberation in 1967 (Elliot-Cooper, 2023). In corporate America, there is a persistent challenge that affects the lives of countless individuals. It manifests in various ways, from biased hiring practices to unequal opportunities for career advancement. As Better defines it, "institutional racism is the 'patterns, procedures, practices, and policies' that function within institutions to intentionally 'penalize, disadvantage, and exploit racialized persons (Omar et al. 2024, as cited in Better 2008, p. 11). As someone who has spent years navigating the corporate landscape, I have seen the impact of these systemic issues firsthand--especially once I became a leader. It is frustrating and heartbreaking to witness talented individuals being overlooked simply because of their skin color or background. This is not just a personal issue; it is a concern that should motivate us to change the very fabric of our workplaces and the culture we create. I remember when I was dealing with a leader who harbored biases and discrimination, always gave me a tough time when African American individuals were up for promotion opportunities. I used to have to "go to war" to get these talented and deserving individuals promoted. The emotional toll of this constant battle was immense, and it often left me feeling drained and disillusioned. It, however, was an evident difference when Caucasian individuals were up for promotion. It was business as usual. I have also seen pay inequities. This leader always championed Caucasians to make more money while taking away from African Americans in raises, bonuses, and initial salary offers. This racist Caucasian leader also was found to have racist social media post one including her in a shirt that said "uppity negro" on it which is very offensive to African Americans. When presenting this to human resources they failed to do anything about it, but offer protection to the racist leader. It was in this moment that I realized the overall systematic structure in corporate America overwhelmingly does not care about African Americans and our overall experiences. Studies have shown that Black workers are paid less and work under worse conditions than their White counterparts (Elliot-Cooper, 2023). In these instances, I started to see the actual inner workings of corporate America. This leader clearly showed biases and discriminatory acts towards African Americans. I then had an aha moment and realized many leaders subtly did.

Despite some disappointing practices that some leaders practice this is where the concept of integrity in leadership comes into play.

Leaders who possess integrity understand that their actions set the tone for the entire organization. They recognize that encouraging an inclusive workplace is not just about meeting diversity quotas; it's about creating a culture where everyone feels valued and empowered. A leader with integrity actively seeks to address the systemic issues that contribute to institutionalized racism, making a concerted effort to educate themselves and their teams on these important topics.

Creating safe spaces for dialogue is another aspect of integrity in leadership. I recall participating in a diversity workshop where employees were invited to share their experiences and feelings about race in the workplace. These conversations were often uncomfortable but necessary. Honest discussions allowed us to be vulnerable, confront biases, and learn from each other. Mentorship programs play a significant role in breaking down barriers as well. Leaders who actively mentor individuals from underrepresented groups help equip them with the tools and networks they need to advance in their careers. I've seen the positive impact of such programs, where mentees have gone on to secure promotions and leadership roles. This benefits the individuals involved and enriches the organization as a whole by bringing diverse perspectives to the forefront.

Ultimately, addressing institutionalized racism in corporate America requires a collective commitment from leaders who are willing to act with integrity. It's not enough to acknowledge the existence of these issues; leaders must take proactive steps to dismantle the systems that uphold them. This is a critical and urgent commitment, about creating a culture where every employee feels seen, heard, and valued.

It's about striving for a workplace that reflects our society's diversity and recognizes all individuals' unique contributions.

Although the fight against institutionalized racism is ongoing, it is worth the effort to keep it at the forefront to induce change. It's a continuous battle that requires our sustained effort and vigilance. It begins with leaders who are willing to take a stand. By embodying integrity and advocating for diversity and inclusion, they can create workplaces that succeed in business and contribute positively to the organization. Together, we can build a corporate America that equips all individuals to thrive, regardless of their race or background.

Chapter 10:
The Role of Whistleblowers

Whistleblowers, the unsung heroes of the corporate world, are not just employees but are brave individuals who step forward to expose fraud, corruption, or unethical practices within their organizations (Chordiya et al., 2020). Their actions, often at the risk of their careers, reputations, and sometimes even their safety, are a powerful testament to the importance of integrity in the workplace.

At its core, integrity is about doing the right thing, even when it is complicated. In many countries, whistleblowing fights corruption (Chordiya et al., 2020). Whistleblowers embody this trait by choosing to speak out against practices they know are wrong. They recognize that remaining silent would compromise their values and enable harmful behavior affecting countless others—employees, customers, and the public. By bringing issues to light, whistleblowers uphold ethical standards and contribute to a culture of accountability.

The relationship between whistleblowing and integrity is profound. When an organization encourages whistleblowing and protects those who come forward, it sends a clear message about its commitment to ethical behavior. This environment cultivates trust, as employees feel permitted to voice their concerns without fear of retaliation. When whistleblowers face backlash or are ignored, it may create a culture of silence where unethical behavior will thrive. This will ultimately damage the organization's integrity. This underscores the significant role whistleblowers play in shaping organizational culture.

Edward Snowden is one of the most notable whistleblower cases in recent years. In 2013, Snowden, a former National Security Agency (NSA) contractor, leaked classified information about the agency's extensive surveillance programs (Edward, 2014). He revealed that the NSA collected vast amounts of data on individuals' phone calls and internet usage without their knowledge or consent, raising significant concerns about privacy rights and government overreach. Snowden's leaks sparked a global debate about national security, civil liberties, and the balance between privacy and surveillance. While some praised him as a hero for exposing government practices, they deemed it unethical, others criticized him for compromising national security. When asked, Snowden stated that he did it because spying is illegal and immoral. In an interview with *The Guardian,* he stated, "My sole motive is to inform the public as to what is done in their name and that which is done against them (Who, 2014). His case remains a pivotal moment in discussions about whistleblowing, transparency, and the responsibilities of government agencies in the digital age.

Whistleblowers challenge the status quo and remind us of the importance of standing up for what is right. They highlight the need for transparency and ethical conduct, serving as an important check on power. In a world where the line between right and wrong can often seem blurred, their courage reinforces the idea that integrity is not just a personal value but a collective responsibility that can lead to meaningful change. Their actions bring to light the importance of transparency in maintaining ethical conduct.

Chapter 11:
Human Resources Ethical Compass

In any organization, human resources (HR) are the backbone for upholding a culture of integrity and ethical behavior. They are not merely the gatekeepers of hiring and compliance but the architects of an environment where honesty and transparency should thrive. In Fortune's *Top 100 Companies*, the top traits they had in common were caring for their employees and having open communication (Hinkin & Tracey, 2010). Integrity should be embedded into the fabric of organizations, and HR should create that foundation. Following this encourages employees to act responsibly and with moral clarity. This pivotal role requires HR professionals to uphold ethical standards and lead by example, demonstrating ethical practices in their daily activities and decision-making processes. When HR fails to follow the policies, it damages potential victims of unethical conduct and puts a stain on HR, causing employees to lose trust and faith in the system. Organizations need to remember this. I have personal accounts where HR failed to uphold the policies that the organization had in place. Human Resources failed to take the correct action because the toxic leaders had "friends in high places." Realizing this discouraged me and confirmed that those policies are thrown out the window depending on who you are. Nevertheless, these casualties do not have to come to a realization. HR needs to prioritize integrity. Doing so will send a powerful message that ethical behavior is valued and expected, inspiring others to follow suit.

The proactive role of human resources in promoting integrity within the organization is vital. Lapses in integrity, whether by one person or many, can compromise employee trust (Mariscotti, 2020). One of the proactive measures HR takes is implementing targeted training and developmental programs. The Federal Sentencing Guidelines recommend that organizations establish an organizational structure that encourages ethical behavior and compliance with the law (Mariscotti, 2020). This involves the board and management oversight and promoting risks, policies, and procedures. This can be seen in various ways, such as implementing diverse hiring practices, which could include blind recruitment or targeted outreach to underrepresented groups, providing equal opportunities for career advancement, which could involve mentorship programs or performance-based promotions, and fostering a culture of inclusion where all voices are heard and valued. These initiatives are about meeting diversity quotas and creating a workplace where everyone feels respected and empowered. This can be seen as DEI initiatives, with organizations recognizing that nurturing a diverse workplace is all-important for innovation and culture. This commitment to inclusivity is closely tied to integrity, as companies must be sincere in their efforts rather than simply checking boxes to meet DEI requirements. The shift to remote and hybrid work has also transformed corporate culture, challenging leaders to maintain trust and accountability across dispersed teams. By investing in these developmental initiatives, HR enhances individual understanding of integrity and strengthens the organization.

Another fundamental aspect of HR's role in promoting integrity is addressing conflict of interest and nepotism, which often go hand in hand. Employees often encounter situations that challenge their ethical beliefs, and a strong support system is essential for addressing these conflicts. A conflict of interest can occur in many forms, such as accepting gifts from a potential client or a manager having a romantic relationship with a team member. This can result in favoritism. Favoritism can negatively impact the decision-making process and damage the morale of the overall team (Mariscotti, 2020). HR should establish confidential reporting mechanisms where employees feel safe to voice their concerns without fear of retaliation.

Nepotism refers to employing family members or friends regardless of merit, skills, preparation, or experience (Mariscotti, 2020). This practice risks impairing objectivity. Organizations should avoid conflict of interests and nepotism as it sends a clear message that their devotion lies in integrity and doing what is right. Nepotism takes many forms in the workplace, including hiring a family member for a position, promoting a friend over a more qualified candidate, giving pay raises to relatives, and assigning favorable tasks to close associates (Verasai, 2022). Nepotism poses a serious ethical dilemma. HR is tasked with creating policies that promote fairness and equal opportunity, but when nepotism leaks into hiring or promotion practices, it contradicts those principles. HR may find itself in a risky position—caught between the demands of leadership and the needs of the broader workforce. While it is natural to want to support family members or close friends, introducing nepotism into the workplace can lead to significant issues that affect morale and the overall integrity of leadership and human resources. One of the most immediate impacts of nepotism is the erosion of trust among employees. When team members perceive that favoritism is at play, it can cause feelings of resentment and decreased productivity (Verasai, 2022). Imagine working hard for a promotion only to see a less qualified relative of a manager get the nod simply because of their connection. This can lead to a toxic atmosphere where employees feel demotivated and undervalued, ultimately affecting productivity and engagement.

Nepotism can undermine the integrity of leadership. It is not illegal except if it violates anti-discrimination laws, which prohibit discrimination based on factors such as race, gender, or familial relationships (Verasai, 2022). Leaders are expected to be fair and transparent in their practices. Leaders who put personal relationships over merit convey that loyalty to family and friends trumps competence. This can create a culture where mediocrity is tolerated, and the most qualified individuals are overlooked. In my honest opinion, many people in leadership made it there through nepotism and not merit. Oftentimes, they lack the morality and integrity to be an effective leader, so we hear many employees talking about toxic leadership and work environments.

To address the challenges that nepotism may cause, organizations need to establish clear policies and practices that promote transparency and equity. This means implementing objective hiring and promotion processes that prioritize qualifications and performance over personal relationships (Verasai, 2022). Encouraging open communication and cultivating an inclusive work environment will also help prevent feelings of resentment (Verasai, 2022). Organizations can rebuild trust and integrity within their leadership and HR practices by incentivizing an environment where merit is recognized and rewarded.

Navigating the complexities of nepotism requires creating a culture of fairness, transparency, and accountability. Leaders must recognize the implications of their decisions and strive to create an inclusive environment where all employees feel valued and empowered. By prioritizing integrity in leadership and human resources, organizations can mitigate the negative impacts of nepotism and build a strong and more resilient workforce.

Creating an ethical environment in the workplace is essential for fostering trust and collaboration among employees, and HR plays a pivotal role in this process. By actively rejecting nepotism and promoting merit-based practices, HR reassures everyone that fairness is a priority. This ensures that everyone feels valued for their skills and contributions. When employees know that opportunities are awarded based on ability rather than personal connections, it creates a sense of fairness that motivates them to give their best. An ethical workplace not only enhances individual morale but also strengthens the organization, leading to greater innovation and success.

Chapter 12:
Building a Culture of Integrity

It is up to leadership to create a workplace culture that values integrity. This requires a thoughtful approach and practical strategies that everyone can embrace. One of the foundational steps is establishing clear policies that outline the organization's commitment to ethical behavior. Policies should be communicated by leadership and human resources effectively to all employees, ensuring everyone understands the expectations and standards. This should also be spoken about in department meetings. When employees know what is expected of them, they are more likely to align their actions with the organization's values. The organization must follow these policies to create a healthy work environment. Unfortunately, this does not occur often in my personal experience. Due to nepotism, systematic racism, misogyny, and other injustices, violations of these policies are frequently swept under the rug, and the victims are made to feel like the problem. However, there is hope. Organizations have the power to change from the top down, inspiring a new era of workplace culture. Until that happens, this vicious cycle will continue to repeat itself.

Another vital aspect of championing integrity is the active involvement of leadership. incorporating regular, self-paced training sessions that each employee attests to is a significant step. These sessions help reinforce the importance of integrity and ethical behavior in everyday work situations. The training programs, which should include real-life scenarios, provide a platform for employees to navigate ethical dilemmas in the work environment. However, leadership's role in speaking about integrity in departmental meetings and town halls truly drives this message home. Their consistent emphasis on integrity keeps the conversation alive and encourages employees to think critically about their decisions, thereby shaping a culture of integrity within the organization.

Open communication channels are significant for supporting a culture of trust. Employees should feel comfortable discussing their concerns and asking questions without fear of retribution. This includes creating safe spaces where employees can voice their thoughts on ethical practices and share feedback about the workplace environment.

Employee feedback and engagement are pivotal in creating a culture of trust. Gaining your teams' confidence is an ongoing effort and is often accomplished by leadership remaining transparent and actively working on barriers in processes and procedures. As leaders, you encourage employees to share their ideas and concerns without fear of retaliation. A proactive approach allows employees' voices to be heard and signals that their input matters. When employees feel heard and valued, they are more likely to take ownership of their roles and contribute positively to the workplace. Through monthly one-on-one sessions, leaders can actively seek feedback from those employees who feel comfortable. Two-way communication will strengthen the sense of belonging while encouraging everyone to uphold the values of integrity within the organization. By implementing these strategies, organizations can nurture a workplace culture prioritizing integrity, ultimately leading to a more ethical and productive environment.

Chapter 13: The Future of Integrity in Corporate America

Corporate America's landscape is poised for significant transformation, particularly regarding integrity in the workplace. Emerging trends suggest that integrity will not just be an organizational goal but a fundamental expectation in the eyes of consumers and employees alike. With that being said, race plays a significant role in issues of fairness and diversity in corporate America- which can also impact ethical decision making and integrity.

Historically speaking, the legacy of discrimination and inequality has shaped the experience and opportunities available for different racial groups. Oftentimes, when a person of color gets a leadership position, it is merely to check a box to meet diversity and inclusion requirements, but there is no respect given once in that leadership position. This happened to me. I had the title of manager; however, the toxic racist boss never respected me or let me make any decisions. I was the face of the team and was there for HR purposes. My experience is not unique. It's a reflection of the larger issue of tokenism in leadership. Retention rates for Black males in leadership positions are often short-lived due to a lack of support and facilitative structures (Wicker, 2021). Organizations need more people of color at the top, not just for the sake of diversity, but to truly understand and address these individual experiences. According to a research study conducted by Interpublic Group (IPG), Black professionals are more likely than White professionals to be more ambitious and have strong networks. However, Black professionals hold only 3.2% of all senior or executive roles and only 1% of all Fortune 500 CEO roles (IPG, 2019). In this same study, Black professionals also experienced racial prejudice at 58% while White professionals were at 15%. Diversity in teams brings various perspectives that can enhance creativity and problem-solving.

A concerning thing that I saw was the toxic leader practicing implicit biases. Implicit biases can influence hiring and promotion decisions where marginalized candidates are often overlooked. This perpetuates cycles of inequality and limits access to leadership roles. Not having diversity in organizations can also impact the company culture, leading to a homogenous company culture that may not be welcoming or inclusive for all employees. A study conducted by Cornelius in 2013 found that four repressive structures can constrain the career development of Black males, which include stereotypes, subjective and unequal career development practices, differentiated opportunities for the acquisition of sociopolitical capital, and shifting priorities in workplace diversity (Wicker, 2021). This can also impact employee retention and fulfilment, particularly amongst underrepresented groups. Leaders within these organizations must strive to be honest and have integrity. Yes, a policy and procedure may be in place, but without the leaders enforcing them and following them, they are null and void. With the growing demand for transparency, organizations must prioritize integrity, setting themselves apart in a crowded landscape.

Globalization only adds to this dynamic as businesses operate across diverse cultures and regulatory environments. The core principles of global strategy, a reliable compass in navigating turbulent environments- help business leaders while aiding growth and innovation, lowering costs, and diversifying risk (Altman & Bastian, 2023). This interconnectedness requires companies to adopt a universal standard of integrity that respects local customs while upholding ethical principles. Additionally, the changing demographics of the workforce—comprising a blend of experienced professionals and fresh talent—bring new perspectives on integrity. There is increasing pressure from both regulators and society for companies to demonstrate their commitment of diversity and inclusion. Failing to address these issues can result in reputational damage.

The good news is that younger generations (millennials and Gen Z) are progressively mindful of corporate ethics and are more likely to align with organizations that demonstrate a genuine commitment to integrity. Both generations value honesty and transparency in their interactions. Editor-in-chief of Bloomberg News, John Micklethwait, once said, "Millennials, more so than any previous generation, understand the importance of ideas. It is immediately obvious to them that they work in a knowledge economy (Moore, 2023)." They not only value but demand open communication and are likely to call out dishonesty and unethical behavior. They value collaboration and inclusivity, striving to create environments where diverse perspectives are acknowledged and respected. Both generations long to find a purpose to be a part of something bigger than themselves

(Moore, 2023). This approach encourages integrity by ensuring that everyone has a voice. In the workplace, they also seek organizations that uphold ethical standards. They support a culture of accountability. Their influence is significant, as they are shaping the future of corporate ethics. Envisioning a future where integrity is at the forefront of corporate culture, we can anticipate a shift where ethical practices become ingrained in every decision, creating workplaces that thrive economically and contribute positively to society.

Looking ahead, it is clear that race, globalization, and the values of Gen Z and Millennials are set to reshape the corporate landscape in profound ways. These generations are passionate about diversity and social justice, pushing companies to embrace and reflect different cultures in their leadership and practices. Globalization brings a wealth of perspectives, and young professionals recognize that diverse teams drive innovation and success. They are also not afraid to hold leaders accountable, with a strong demand for transparency and ethical behavior. Ultimately, this shift will create more inclusive and adaptable workplaces that align with the values of a new generation eager to make a difference.

Chapter 14: Taking Action

It is important to remember that integrity in the workplace benefits employees and organizations. Integrity is a lofty ideal and a practical necessity that significantly shapes our organizational culture. It enhances the employee experience, drives success, and, most importantly, is a key factor in creating a positive work environment. When organizations commit to ethical behavior and prioritize integrity, they build trust, enhance collaboration, and ensure high employee morale. Taking action to uphold integrity and ethical behavior in corporate America starts with a commitment at every level of an organization. It's not just about having a code of ethics on paper; it's about embedding those principles into the company culture. Leaders must model ethical behavior, demonstrating transparency and accountability in decision-making. When employees see their leaders acting with integrity, it creates a ripple effect, encouraging them to uphold those same values in their daily interactions.

Communication is another fundamental piece of the puzzle. I firmly believe that creating an environment where everyone feels safe to voice their concerns is vital for nurturing integrity. In my experience, organizations that prioritize open dialogue tend to thrive. I've been part of teams where we held regular discussions and transparency from leaders instilled trust, which helped us navigate tough situations and strengthened our bonds as colleagues. However, I've also experienced the opposite: a lack of transparency, favoritism, and a toxic work environment brought on by a leader. This underscores the importance of open communication. When people feel heard, they are more likely to act in the company's and each other's best interests.

It is necessary to integrate ethical standards into hiring and promotion practices. It's not just about skills and experience; it's also about finding individuals who resonate with the company's values. I've seen teams flourish when they consist of members who are not only talented but also genuinely care about doing what's right. Working alongside people who share my integrity commitment motivates me to uphold those standards and encourages a collective sense of responsibility. Leaders and HR professionals play a crucial role in this, as they are the ones who set the tone for the company's culture. They need to check their biases to ensure fair hiring and firing practices. Any form of discrimination, including moving the goalpost or targeting employees based on their race, is unethical and should be promptly addressed if it becomes a pattern. Remember that employees are more likely to feel appreciated and act ethically when they observe equal opportunities and their contributions are valued and acknowledged.

Promoting integrity and ethical behavior in the corporate world is not a task for a few, but a collective effort. It's about fostering a culture where integrity is not just a value, but a celebrated and rewarded practice. When employees are empowered to make choices that align with their values, and when companies prioritize trust, openness, and shared responsibility, they can enhance their reputations and cultivate an engaged, motivated, and proud workforce. This is the essence of an ethical organization.

Now is the time for action. I urge you to make a firm commitment to integrity in your professional life. Whether you are a leader or an individual contributor, your choices matter. As a leader, you have a unique opportunity to set examples in daily interactions and advocate for transparency and accountability, permitting others to do the same. Your leadership can inspire others to uphold the highest ethical standards. To further engage with this critical topic, consider exploring additional resources such as books, articles, and workshops focused on ethics and integrity. Corporate America can be a place where integrity is not merely a concept but a living, breathing part of corporate America, enriching our workplaces and lives.

Chapter 15:
My Final Thoughts As An I/O Psychologist

As I reflect on my career as a leader in corporate America and an industrial and organizational psychologist, I realize that integrity is a fundamental principle in the workplace. Integrity isn't simply about following rules; it's about creating an environment where employees feel safe and valued. I've seen how leaders who genuinely embody ethical behavior inspire trust and commitment among their teams. When integrity is at the core of an organization's culture, it encourages open communication and collaboration, allowing individuals to thrive and contribute their best work.

I've also witnessed instances where unethical behavior has undermined this culture, particularly from those in leadership positions. Experiencing this firsthand left me in a state of shock and very saddened by this behavior. I recall situations where leaders made decisions that prioritized race and friendships over the well-being of all employees, creating a toxic and hostile work environment. Seeing how these actions can travel through an organization, eroding trust and morale, is disheartening. Such experiences have reinforced my belief that ethical leadership and having integrity cannot just be a talking point, but something that all leaders live by.

Human Resources plays a pivotal role in shaping an organization's ethical landscape. HR professionals are often responsible for implementing policies that pushes for fairness and inclusivity. I've seen how effective HR practices can lead to a more equitable workplace, but I've also encountered situations where HR has fallen short. In some cases, I've seen HR personnel overlook unethical behavior from leadership, allowing the cycle of abusive and unethical behavior to continue. This complicity can perpetuate a culture of silence, where the victims feel unsafe to voice their concerns or report misconduct.

Addressing race and biases in the workplace is another critical aspect of championing integrity. Despite progress in many areas, systemic issues often persist, impacting experiences of employees from diverse backgrounds. I've observed how unconscious biases can seep into hiring practices and performance evaluations, leading to inequities that hinder the growth of underrepresented groups. It is key for organizations to actively confront these biases and commit to creating a more inclusive environment where everyone has an equal opportunity to succeed.

Creating this environment requires ongoing training and open dialogue around race and equity. Organizations must encourage conversations that allow employees to share their experiences and perspectives. The critical component is leaders have to practice what they preach. Being hypocritical does not benefit the employees or the organization. When individuals feel heard and understood, they have a sense of belonging and are empowered to contribute fully. I've seen firsthand how organizations that embrace inclusivity and diversity not only enhance employee satisfaction but also drive innovation and success.

Integrity and ethical leadership are vital components of a thriving workplace, and HR has a crucial role in supporting these values. However, it's indispensable to remain vigilant against unethical behavior, whether from leaders or within HR. As an industrial and organizational psychologist, I am committed to helping organizations navigate these challenges and nurtures cultures that prioritize ethics, inclusivity, and fairness. I look forward to continuing this important work and contributing to environments where everyone can thrive and feel valued.

References

Alfonseca, K. (2023, February 10). DEI: What does it mean and what is its purpose? *ABC News.* https://abcnews.go.com/US/dei-programs/story?id=97004455

Altman, S. A., & Bastian, C. R. (2023, July 11). The State of Globalization in 2023. *Harvard Business Review.* https://hbr.org/2023/07/the-state-of-globalization-in-2023

Arcadi, T. (2020). Risk and ruin: Enron and the culture of American capitalism by Gavin Benke (review). *Enterprise & Society, 21*(1), 311-313.

Bizadmin. (2023, July 8). Navigating the Ethical Decision Making Process: A Guide for Ethical Dillemas. *Business Ethics Network.* https://www.businessethicsnetwork.org/navigating-the-ethical-decision-making-process-a-guide-for-ethical-dilemmas/#Key_Components_of_Ethical_Decision-Making

Carbo, J. A. (2017). *Understanding, defining and eliminating workplace bullying: Assuring dignity at work* (1st ed.). Routledge. https://doi.org/10.4324/9781315549057

Carle, M. (2023). *Walk away to win: a playbook to combat workplace bullying* (1st ed.). McGraw Hill.

Chordiya, R., Sabharwal, M., Relly, J. E., & Berman, E. M. (2020). Organizational protection for whistleblowers: A cross-national study. *Public Management Review, 22*(4), 527-552. https://doi.org/10.1080/14719037.2019.1599058

Colquitt, J. A., & Baer, M. D. (2023). Foster trust through ability, benevolence, and integrity. *Principles of Organizational Behavior: The Handbook of Evidence-Based Management 3rd Edition*, 345-363.

Edward Snowden: Leaks that exposed US spy programme. (2014, January 17). *BBC News*. https://www.bbc.com/news/world-us-canada-23123964

Elliott-Cooper, A. (2023). Abolishing institutional racism. *Race & Class, 65*(1), 100-118. https://doi.org/10.1177/03063968231166901

Ete, Z., Epitropaki, O., Zhou, Q., & Graham, L. (2022). Leader and organizational behavioral integrity and follower behavioral outcomes: The role of identification processes. *Journal of Business Ethics, 176*(4), 741-760. https://doi.org/10.1007/s10551-020-04728-6

Hinkin, T. R., & Tracey, J. B. (2010). What makes it so great?: An analysis of human resources practices among Fortune's best companies to work for. *Cornell Hospitality Quarterly, 51*(2), 158-170. https://doi.org/10.1177/1938965510362487

IPG sponsors new study on being black in corporate America (2019). Disco Digital Media, Inc.

J.R.C. Pimentel, Kuntz, J. R., & Elenkov, D. S. (2010). Ethical decision-making: an integrative model for business practice. *European Business Review, 22*(4), 359-376. https://doi.org/10.1108/09555341011056159

Klahn Acuña, B., & Male, T. (2022). Toxic leadership and academics' work engagement in higher education: A cross-sectional study from Chile. Educational Management, Administration & Leadership, 174114322210844. https://doi.org/10.1177/17411432221084474

Mariscotti, E. E. (2020). *Corporate risks and leadership: What every executive should know about risks, ethics, compliance and human resources* (1st;1;1st; ed.). Routledge. https://doi.org/10.4324/9781003038238

Miazad, A. (2020). Sex, power, and corporate governance. *UC Davis L. Rev., 54*, 1913.

Moore, K. (2023). *Generation why: how boomers can lead and learn from millennials and gen Z* (1st ed.). McGill-Queen's University Press.

Nasim, M. A., Yadav, R. S., Dash, S. S., & Bamel, U. (2023). Leadership styles and safety culture – a meta-analytic study. *International Journal of Organizational Analysis (2005), 31*(7), 3233-3250. https://doi.org/10.1108/IJOA-02-2022-3166

Omar, S., Williams, C. C., Bugg, L. B., & Colantonio, A. (2024). "somewhere along the line, your mask isn't going to be fitting right": Institutional racism in black narratives of traumatic brain injury rehabilitation across the practice continuum. *BMC Health*

Services Research, *24*(1), 834-24. https://doi.org/10.1186/s12913-024-10986-1

Schreane, K. C. (2021). *Corporations compassion culture: Leading your business toward diversity, equity, and inclusion* (1st ed.). Wiley.

Sims, R. R. (1992). The challenge of ethical behavior in organizations. *Journal of Business Ethics, 11*(7), 505-513. https://doi.org/10.1007/BF00881442

Thornton-Lugo, M. A., & Cubrich, M. (2021). Ethical dilemmas and the victim's perspective: Broadening ethics in industrial-organizational psychology. *Industrial and Organizational Psychology, 14*(3), 345-349. https://doi.org/10.1017/iop.2021.69

Verasai, A. (2022, December 24). Is Nepotism in the Workplace Illegal in America? *The HR Digest*. https://www.thehrdigest.com/is-nepotism-in-the-workplace-illegal-in-america/

Who is Edward Snowden, the Man Who Spilled the NSA's Secrets. (2014, May 26). *NBC News*. https://www.nbcnews.com/feature/edward-snowden-interview/who-edward-snowden-man-who-spilled-nsas-secrets-n114861

Wicker, C. J. (2021). The trenches and valleys of corporate America: A black male human resource Leader's autoethnographic account. *Advances in Developing Human Resources, 23*(4), 335-353. https://doi.org/10.1177/15234223211037762

Woiceshyn, J. (2011). A model for ethical decision making in business: Reasoning, intuition, and rational moral principles. *Journal of Business Ethics, 104*(3), 311-323. https://doi.org/10.1007/s10551-011-0910-1

Zablow, R. J. (2006). Creating and sustaining an ethical workplace. *Risk Management, 53*(9), 26.

About the Author

Shanesha Scott, a passionate industrial and organizational psychologist, is an experienced leader in corporate America. Her motivation to write this book stems from her deep concern over the lack of integrity she has witnessed in various professional environments. Shanesha firmly believes that integrity is not just a buzzword but a fundamental quality that every ethical leader must embody. Her insights and experiences aim to instill this belief in others, encouraging them to prioritize ethical practices in their careers and personal lives. Shanesha's professional life is one of many areas in which she excels. She is also a dedicated advocate, partnering with End Workplace Abuse to promote psychologically safe workplaces. Their goal is to pass the Workplace Psychological Safety Act in all 50 states. Shanesha's commitment to making a positive impact in her community and globally is evident in her diverse interests. In her free time, she treasures time spent with her family and nurtures her creative side as the proud owner of her clothing boutique, Fad Fashions. Here, she combines her love for fashion with her entrepreneurial spirit.

Please visit www.shaneshascott.com to check out all her endeavors.

www.ingramcontent.com/pod-product-compliance
Lightning Source LLC
Chambersburg PA
CBHW030048230526
45471CB00003B/1000